Kentucky

A Buddy Book
by
Julie Murray

ABDO
Publishing Company

VISIT US AT
www.abdopub.com

Published by ABDO Publishing Company, 4940 Viking Drive, Edina, Minnesota 55435.

Printed in the United States.

Edited by: Sarah Tieck
Contributing Editor: Michael P. Goecke
Graphic Design: Deb Coldiron, Maria Hosley
Image Research: Sarah Tieck
Photographs: Brand X Pictures, Clipart.com, Digital Vision, Getty Images, Library of Congress, One Mile Up, PhotoDisc, Photos.com. Special thanks to the National Scenic Byways Program (www.byways.org) for use of the photos on pages 6 and 23.

Library of Congress Cataloging-in-Publication Data

Murray, Julie, 1969-
    Kentucky / Julie Murray.
        p. cm. — (The United States)
    Includes bibliographical references and index.
    ISBN 1-59197-676-6
        1. Kentucky—Juvenile literature. I. Title.

F451.3.M87 2005
976.9—dc22

                                                        2004066016

Table Of Contents

A Snapshot Of Kentucky 4

Where Is Kentucky? 7

Fun Facts .10

Cities And The Capital 12

Famous Citizens 14

Land Of Horses 16

Appalachian Mountains 20

Mammoth Cave 24

A History Of Kentucky 28

A State Map 30

Important Words 31

Web Sites .31

Index 32

A Snapshot Of Kentucky

Kentucky is known as the "Bluegrass State." The name comes from a type of grass that grows in Kentucky. This grass is called Kentucky Bluegrass. In the spring, the grass grows small, bluish blossoms that make the ground look light blue.

There are 50 states in the United States. Every state is different. Every state has an official state nickname.

Kentucky is known for its horses.

A natural bridge in Kentucky.

Kentucky became the 15th state on June 1, 1792. Kentucky has 40,411 square miles (104,664 sq km). It is the 37th-largest state in the United States. Kentucky is home to 4,041,769 people.

Where Is Kentucky?

There are four parts of the United States. Each part is called a region. Each region is in a different area of the country. The United States Census Bureau says the four regions are the Northeast, the South, the Midwest, and the West.

Kentucky is in the South region of the United States. Kentucky has mild weather. Summers are warm, and winters are cool. It also rains a lot in Kentucky.

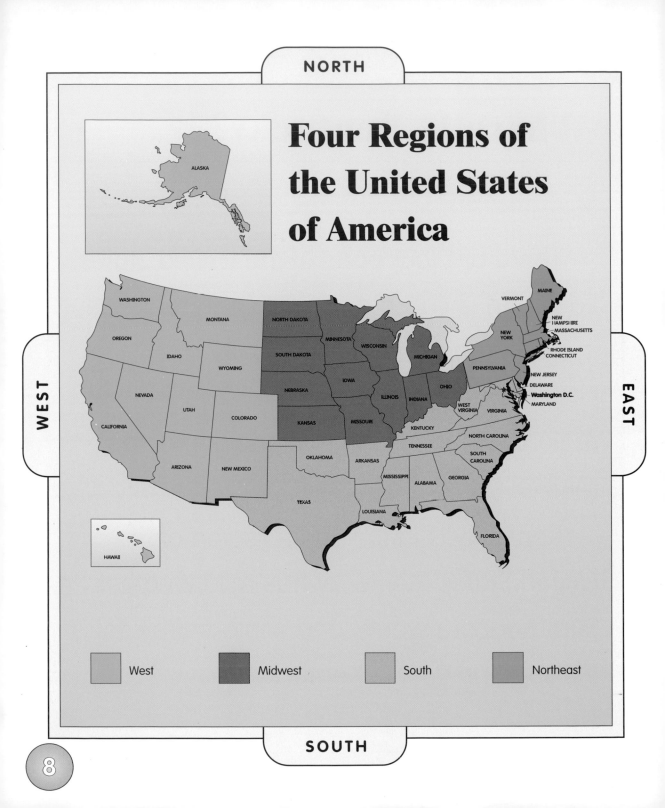

Four Regions of the United States of America

NORTH

WEST

EAST

SOUTH

ALASKA

WASHINGTON
OREGON
IDAHO
MONTANA
NORTH DAKOTA
MINNESOTA
WISCONSIN
SOUTH DAKOTA
MICHIGAN
WYOMING
NEVADA
UTAH
COLORADO
NEBRASKA
IOWA
ILLINOIS
INDIANA
OHIO
CALIFORNIA
ARIZONA
NEW MEXICO
KANSAS
MISSOURI
KENTUCKY
WEST VIRGINIA
VIRGINIA
OKLAHOMA
ARKANSAS
TENNESSEE
NORTH CAROLINA
SOUTH CAROLINA
TEXAS
MISSISSIPPI
ALABAMA
GEORGIA
LOUISIANA
FLORIDA
VERMONT
MAINE
NEW HAMPSHIRE
MASSACHUSETTS
NEW YORK
RHODE ISLAND
CONNECTICUT
PENNSYLVANIA
NEW JERSEY
DELAWARE
Washington D.C.
MARYLAND
HAWAII

West
Midwest
South
Northeast

8

Kentucky is bordered by seven other states. Tennessee is to the south. Missouri is to the west. Illinois, Indiana, and Ohio are to the north. West Virginia and Virginia are to the east.

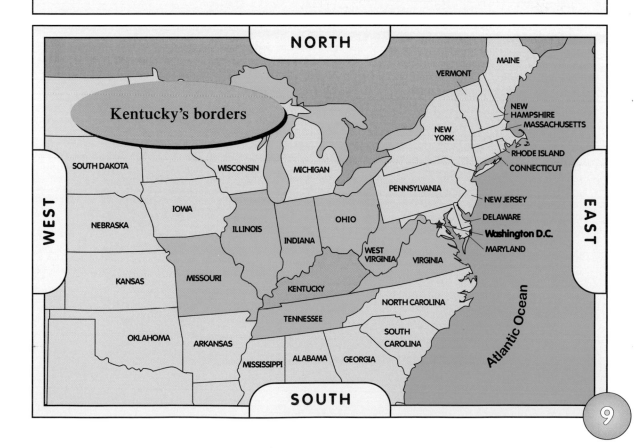

Kentucky

State abbreviation: KY

State nickname: Bluegrass State

State capital: Frankfort

State motto: United we stand, divided we fall.

Statehood: June 1, 1792, 15th state

Population: 4,041,769, ranks 25th

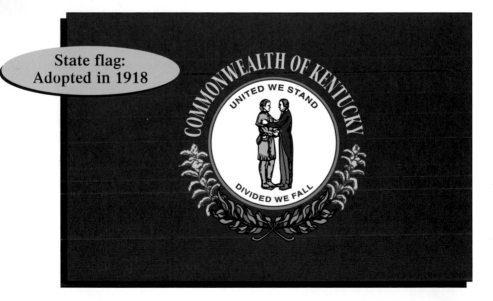

State flag:
Adopted in 1918

Land area: 40,411 square miles (104,664 sq km), ranks 37th

State tree: Kentucky coffee tree

State song: "My Old Kentucky Home"

State government: Three branches: legislative, executive, and judicial

Average July temperature: 77°F (25°C)

Average January temperature: 34°F (1°C)

State flower: Goldenrod

State bird: Cardinal

State wild animal: Gray squirrel

Cities And The Capital

Lexington is the largest city in Kentucky. It is home to 260,512 people. It was named for a famous battle that happened in Massachusetts during the American Revolutionary War. Today, people go to Lexington to buy race horses. Tobacco is also an important product grown in Lexington.

Frankfort is the capital city of Kentucky. It is located in the northern part of the state. Frankfort is not a big city. Only about 27,000 people live there. Frankfort's chief industry is government.

A scenic pathway in Lexington

Famous Citizens

Abraham Lincoln (1809–1865)

In 1809, Abraham Lincoln was born in a log cabin near Hodgenville. There, people can visit a one-room cabin like the one where Lincoln was born. Lincoln is famous for being the 16th United States president. Lincoln became the president on March 4, 1861. He worked hard to end the American Civil War. Lincoln is famous for helping to end slavery, too. He was shot and killed on April 14, 1865.

Abraham Lincoln

Famous Citizens

Muhammad Ali (1942–)

Muhammad Ali

Muhammad Ali was born in Louisville. Ali is one of the most famous boxers to ever live. He won a gold medal in the 1960 Summer Olympics. This launched his professional career as a boxer. He was the heavyweight champion of boxing four times during his career. He retired from boxing in the 1980s.

Land Of Horses

Kentucky is famous for its horses. There are many horse farms in Kentucky. The farmers raise Thoroughbred horses. Thoroughbreds are often used for racing or riding competitions. Thoroughbreds are raised in Kentucky and sold throughout the United States. They are tall, strong horses that can run very fast.

Horses graze in grassy fields like this one.

A jockey riding a horse in the Kentucky Derby.

The Kentucky Derby is a famous horse race. It happens at Churchill Downs in Louisville every May. The first race was in 1875. For more than 130 years, thousands of people have come to see the Kentucky Derby. Before the big race, there is a weeklong festival with parades, fireworks, and concerts.

Appalachian Mountains

The Appalachian Mountains run through southeastern Kentucky. In Kentucky, this area is called the Cumberland Mountains. The state's highest point is Black Mountain. It is 4,145 feet (1,263 m) above sea level.

Cumberland Gap in the Cumberland Mountains.

The Appalachian Mountains are the second-largest mountain range in North America. They stretch for about 1,500 miles (2,414 km) from Quebec, Canada, to Birmingham, Alabama. The only mountain range that is larger is the Rocky Mountains in the western United States.

The Appalachians are known for having lots of coal. Coal is an important product in Kentucky. Workers mine coal from the mountains.

Cumberland Falls State Park

23

Mammoth Cave

Mammoth Cave is part of Mammoth Cave National Park. It is also part of the Mammoth-Flint Ridge Cave System. This is the longest cave system in the world. It is located in west central Kentucky. Mammoth Cave has more than 300 miles (483 km) of passages.

The cave was formed over millions of years as water ran through the limestone. Rivers run through parts of the cave, and animals, such as bats, call Mammoth Cave their home.

Stalactites in a cave in
Mammoth Cave National Park.

This farm is near Mammoth Cave National Park.

Today, around two million people visit Mammoth Cave each year. People can take guided tours through part of the cave system. The cave's temperature is cool. Water drips from the rock formations overhead.

Kentucky

1750: Thomas Walker explores Kentucky.

1767: Famous pioneer Daniel Boone visits Kentucky.

1792: Kentucky becomes the 15th state on June 1.

1863: The famous feud between the Hatfields and the McCoys begins on the border of Kentucky and West Virginia.

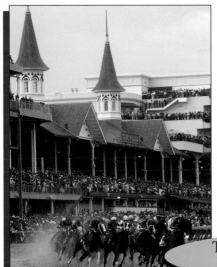

1875: Horses race for the first time at the Kentucky Derby.

1887: Mary Towles Sasseen, a schoolteacher from Henderson, begins celebrating Mother's Day.

The Kentucky Derby happens every year in May.

1930: In Corbin, Colonel Harlan Sanders starts making what will become Kentucky Fried Chicken.

1983: Martha Layne Collins is the first woman elected governor of Kentucky.

2005: Country music legend Loretta Lynn wins several music awards. She is a native of Butcher Hollow.

Loretta Lynn is sometimes called "the queen of country music."

Cities in Kentucky

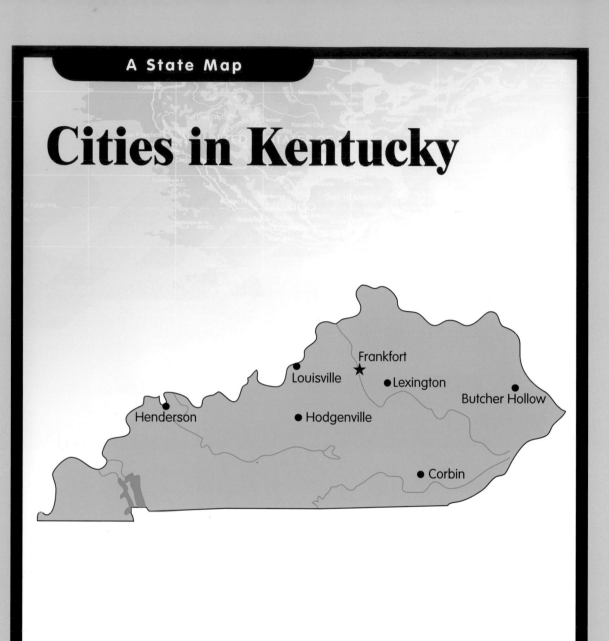

Frankfort

Louisville

Lexington

Butcher Hollow

Henderson

Hodgenville

Corbin

Important Words

American Civil War the United States war between the Northern and the Southern states.

American Revolutionary War Americans fought for freedom from Great Britain in this famous war.

capital a city where government leaders meet.

nickname a name that describes something special about a person or a place.

slavery the owning of people as slaves.

Web Sites

To learn more about Kentucky, visit ABDO Publishing Company on the World Wide Web. Web site links about Kentucky are featured on our Book Links page. These links are routinely monitored and updated to provide the most current information available.

www.abdopub.com

Index

Alabama **22**

Ali, Muhammad **15**

American Civil War **14**

American Revolutionary War **12**

Appalachian Mountains **20, 21, 22, 23**

Black Mountain...........................**20**

bluegrass **4**

Boone, Daniel **28**

Butcher Hollow...................**29, 30**

Canada **22**

Churchill Downs **19**

coal **22**

Collins, Martha Layne **29**

Corbin **29, 30**

Cumberland Falls State Park **23**

Cumberland Gap **21**

Cumberland Mountains **20, 21**

Frankfort...........................**10, 12, 30**

Hatfield (family)..........................**28**

Henderson **29, 30**

Hodgenville **14, 30**

horses.......**5, 12, 16, 17, 18, 19, 28**

Illinois **9**

Indiana **9**

Kentucky Derby **18, 19, 28**

Kentucky Fried Chicken **29**

Lexington **12, 13, 30**

Lincoln, Abraham **14**

Louisville..........................**15, 19, 30**

Lynn, Loretta **29**

Mammoth Cave **24, 25, 26, 27**

Massachusetts **12**

McCoy (family) **28**

Midwest....................................**7, 8**

Missouri......................................**9**

Northeast..................................**7, 8**

Ohio **9**

Rocky Mountains........................**22**

Sanders, Colonel Harlan.............**29**

Sasseen, Mary Towles **29**

South.......................................**7, 8**

Tennessee **9**

United States Census Bureau **7**

Virginia **9**

Walker, Thomas **28**

West.......................................**7, 8**

West Virginia..........................**9, 28**